Mel Bay Presents

JOE PASS
IMPROVISING IDEAS

by Joe Pass & Jude Hibler

Visit us on the Web at www.melbay.com — E-mail us at email@melbay.com

Dedication to ELLEN LUEDERS PASS
In Memorial
JOE PASS
January 13, 1929 - May 23, 1994

In January 1989, **Joe Pass** turned 60 years old. He was playing a gig in San Diego, California. Attending with him was his fiancée, **Ellen Lueders**, a lovely German woman.

Joe was happy and proud to have Ellen with him as he began his San Diego engagement. During the program, he introduced a song that reminded him of his beloved Ellen and dedicated it to her. The song was called Beautiful Love by Victor Young, Haven Gillespie, Wayne King and Egbert van Alstyne.

On May 23, 1994, Joe Pass died. While the loss of Joe as a person is huge, he has left a legacy for generations to come through his recorded music and his music books. I believe that this book was the last one that Joe worked on, which makes it even more special to me.

I, like millions of Joe Pass fans and friends throughout the world, loved him and admired him for his courage in overcoming seemingly insurmountable obstacles, for preserving and promoting our common heritage through jazz, for his sense of humor (often at his own expense) and for his enormous talent through the guitar.

I think Joe would have liked to dedicate this book to Ellen, his Beautiful Love. On his behalf, Mel Bay Publications, publisher William Bay and I dedicate this to Ellen Lueders Pass, Joe's inspiration, friend, wife and Beautiful Love.

Because Joe Pass contributed so vastly to the world of music and jazz particularly, his widow—Ellen Lueders Pass—and I are in the process of co-writing Joe's biography. We are in the data-gathering stage at the time of this printing. If you have information for us, please contact me at (303) 776-1764 or fax it to (303) 678-8343, or mail it to me at 3721 Columbia Drive, Longmont, CO 80503.

Thank You--Jude Hibler

Joe Pass was one of the finest people I have ever met. He was a giant in the field of guitar. He was also a very sensitive, conscientious, and gifted individual. I feel honored to have worked with Joe on his various books. I will treasure his memory.

-William Bay

Photo by Jude Hibler

TABLE OF CONTENTS

Joe Pass Statement

First I want to thank **Jude Hibler** for *"harassing" me into doing this book! If it wasn't for her, this book would never have come about. It was her idea. We put in jazz licks that are traditional: they cover the years of jazz from the early swing years through the bebop years. The traditional jazz licks that are a part of all the jazz players from Louie Armstrong to Chick Corea.

When you are playing for any length of time and you've got the experience, like I did, forty years of experience, you automatically incorporate what you hear other people play into your own style.

What we are trying to do is to pass them on for students to play them. Only those licks that the student likes will stay with him or her.

I hope you enjoy the book and benefit from it. I want to repeat that I am grateful to Jude for doing *all* the work on this book...especially for getting (trumpeter) **Ron Miles** and (guitarist) **Dale Bruning** of Denver for transcribing the jazz licks. I really appreciate their efforts.

Improvising Ideas comes from a collection of swing playing all the way to bebop. Some of them are traditional, while some are a little bit complicated, harmonically, I think, but it's important to try to understand how you decide on what changes to make.

Joe Pass

(*: When I asked Joe to make a statement for this book, we were talking on the telephone. I taped his message and then transcribed it.

He wanted to be sure that I included his thanks to me and I assure you that when he made his first statement, we both laughed very hard! Without hearing him yourself, the reading of his message might seem unappreciative. It is anything but that, believe me. Jude Hibler**)**

About the photographs:

(**Joe Pass** appeared at the *North Sea Jazz Festival* in The Hague, Netherlands in July, 1991. He was in a duo concert with supreme bassist **Niels-Henning Ørsted Pedersen**.
--- Photos by *Jude Hibler*)

About the transcribers:

Dale Bruning: A world-class guitarist, *Mr. Bruning* has lived, played and taught in the Denver area for 30 years. Before that, he lived and worked in Philadelphia. While there, he was the band director for the *Del Shields' Summer Showcase*, a television variety show. In his career, he has played with such artists as *Red Norvo, Jim Hall, Buddy De Franco, Dizzy Gillespie, Specs Wright, Gus Johnson, Marian Mc Partland, Carol Sloane, Nancy Wilson, Jake Hanna, Slide Hampton, Ray Bryant, Spike Robinson, Ellyn Rucker, Lew Tabackin, Bruno Carr, Art Van Damme, Eric Gunnison, Paul Warburton, Art Lande, Ron Washington, Carl Fontana, Dave McKenna, Erroll Garner, Nat Yarbrough, Al Grey, Nelson Boyd, Tony Luis, Jake Hanna, Peanuts Hucko, Ralph Sutton, Phil Urso, Chet Baker, Johnny Smith, Buddy Montgomery* and *Ron Miles*.

While he has had virtually every musician of note in the Denver area study with him, perhaps his most "famous" student was guitarist *Bill Frisell*. Mr. Bruning currently plays in a trio with bassist *Paul Warburton* and trumpeter *Ron Miles*. He and Warburton can be heard on the Capri release called *Paul Warburton/Dale Bruning Duo, Our Delight*. Mr. Bruning is in the process of writing a series of guitar instruction books in collaboration with Jude Hibler, "Dale Bruning's Jazz Guitar Series, Volume I--The Importance of Phrasing and Articulation," will be available at the end of 1994.

Ron Miles: Winning *Down Beat's* Outstanding Student Performance award in 1985, trumpeter Ron Miles is a virtuoso who has also earned awards as Best Trumpeter in the Classical area in the college world for several consecutive years in the mid-'80s. The International Association of Jazz Educators selected him as the Best College Soloist in Colorado in 1984.

He currently is an Assistant Professor of Trumpet at Metropolitan State College of Denver. He is active in Colorado as a composer, leader of his own ensemble, and plays in other groups, such as the trio with *Dale Bruning* and *Paul Warburton*. He has played in the *Duke Ellington Orchestra*, under the leadership of *Mercer Ellington*. His two CD releases, featuring him as the leader, include *Distance for Safety* (Prolific Records) and *Witness* (Capri).)

Jude Hibler Statement

To move from a position of being able to play the necessary two chords on the folk tune *Go Tell Aunt Rhody* on the guitar to authoring a guitar music instruction book in conjunction with one of the greatest guitarists of all time is the ultimate step in irony. I have experienced many feelings and thoughts since beginning this effort. As a novice guitarist, I took a class from Joe in 1987 in San Diego during a *Guitar Masters' Class*. The class ran three to four hours each night for three nights.

I typed up my notes and asked Joe to read them for errors. He liked them and told me to send them to his publisher at *Mel Bay Publications,* **William Bay**. I was so flattered by Joe's attention and by the fact that *Mel Bay* books had been part of my music book library for most of my life that I just nodded my head in a stunned, but affirming way. Meanwhile, Snoopy was dancing for joy on top of my heart!

The realization of the implications of having my name connected with both **Joe Pass** and *Mel Bay Books* did not strike me with full force until this past year when time became critical for completing the task of writing this manuscript. In 1992, I moved from San Diego to Longmont, Colorado...a town forty miles north of Denver. The fortunate blessing in that move was to put me in close proximity to the man who was my first guitar teacher and the first person to unmask some of the mystery that jazz music had always held for me, **Dale Bruning**.

Dale was my first guitar teacher in Denver in 1983. He is a musician who plays the guitar as well as any of the masters he introduced me to, including *Joe Pass, Jim Hall, Kenny Burrell, Barney Kessel, Mundell Lowe, Tal Farlow, Herb Ellis, Cal Collins* and *Ed Bickert*. In the last few months of working on this book, Dale once again became my mentor and educator in the theory and flow of this book. But at the same time, let me quickly add that if there is any lack of clarity in the book, that responsibility is solely mine.

Trumpeter **Ron Miles** transcribed the Joe Pass lines found here and Dale double-checked any of the work that Ron had questions about. Joe and I thank these two men immensely for their assistance.

A two-part goal of mine in presenting this material to you is as follows:
1. To be faithful to the presentation that Joe made to his students in 1987 during his *Guitar Masters' Class*.
2. To present the material as clearly as possible, laying down foundational steps that bridge the essence of theory, to the adaptation of improvisation, to the ultimate experience of playing melodies.

I want to thank both Joe and Bill Bay: Bill, who is a delightful person, for his patience in waiting for this manuscript, for his kindness and for his sense of humor. He serves in his role as publisher with integrity and honor. Thanks, too, for giving me the opportunity to be involved in this project. I appreciate you, Bill.

Working with Joe has been an honor and I am privileged to call him "friend." Thanks, Joe, for sharing your gift of music with the world during your lifetime. Your music provides a legion of material creating a Legend that is Joe Pass.

With love -- Jude Hibler

About the Author:

Jude Hibler was Publisher/Editor of *Jazz Link* magazine from 1988-1991. While the magazine is no longer in print, *Jazz Link Enterprises* provides media services, primarily to jazz-related fields. She is currently a photojournalist whose work appears in *Jazzscene of Oregon; Concord Jazz* records publicity/promotions; and is collaborating with guitarist **Dale Bruning** in writing a series of guitar instruction books. The first one, *Dale Bruning's Jazz Guitar Series Volume I— The Importance of Phrasing and Articulation,* will be available at the end of 1994.

She has annotated liner notes for CDs and was a contributing writer to the soon-to-be-released *Encyclopedia of Jazz* book (Oxford University Press), edited by **Leonard Feather** and **Ira Gitler**.

She can be reached at: Jazz Link Enterprises, 3721 Columbia Drive, Longmont, CO 80503; (303) 776-1764; FAX (303) 678-8343.

INTRODUCTION

Music is composed of three elements:
- melody
- harmony
- rhythm

This music book is *not* a theory book. That is, in order for the student to learn about chords, scales, intervals and the other elements of music that make it rich, you need to study music theory. There are several *Mel Bay* books available for this.

What this book will provide you with, however, is a map that guides you to *Joe Pass Improvisational Practice Techniques* which encompass the three basic elements of music.

There is no short cut for learning scales, chord structures and intervals. The better your understanding of these components, the easier improvising becomes.

To begin with, this book will introduce you to the *Joe Pass Chord Forms* that he uses in teaching situations. Then one example of various scale forms will be written out, using the key of C throughout those examples. These foundational tools will lead to the *Joe Pass Improvisational Practice Techniques*. These will be followed by some *Joe Pass Jazz Lines* that he designed specifically for this book. Lastly, an original song by Joe Pass, *Jude's Blues*, is included as an example of how you assemble all of the music ingredients and the practice techniques into actually playing and improvising on a melody.

MAJOR KEY SIGNATURES	THE CYCLE OF KEYS

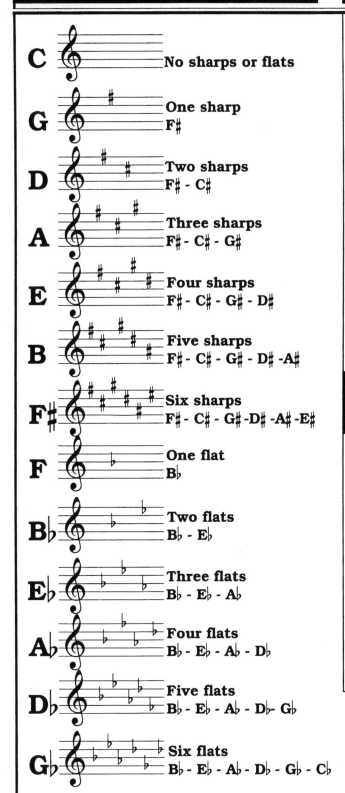

C	No sharps or flats
G	One sharp F♯
D	Two sharps F♯ - C♯
A	Three sharps F♯ - C♯ - G♯
E	Four sharps F♯ - C♯ - G♯ - D♯
B	Five sharps F♯ - C♯ - G♯ - D♯ -A♯
F♯	Six sharps F♯ - C♯ - G♯ -D♯ -A♯ -E♯
F	One flat B♭
B♭	Two flats B♭ - E♭
E♭	Three flats B♭ - E♭ - A♭
A♭	Four flats B♭ - E♭ - A♭ - D♭
D♭	Five flats B♭ - E♭ - A♭ - D♭- G♭
G♭	Six flats B♭ - E♭ - A♭ - D♭ - G♭ - C♭

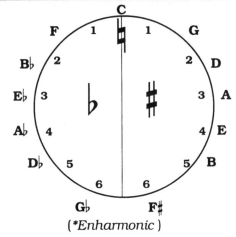

(*Enharmonic)

Going around the circle clockwise will take us through the **Dominant keys.**

Going around the circle counterclockwise will take us through the **Sub-Dominant keys.**

* *Enharmonic:* Written differently as to notation but sounding the same.

The Major and Relative Minor Keys

MAJOR KEYS	RELATIVE MINOR KEYS
C	Am
G	Em
D	Bm
A	F♯m
E	C♯m
B	G♯m
F♯	D♯m
F	Dm
B♭	Gm
E♭	Cm
A♭	Fm
D♭	B♭m
G♭	E♭m

MUSIC COMPONENTS

For the next several pages, you will find the essential elements required to make music: chords and scales. Many guitar books spell out literally thousands of chords. However, most masters of the guitar concentrate on selected chords that *sound* good to them. *Sound* is what Joe Pass emphasizes again and again.

Within the variations of chords are *chord inversions and chord substitutions. Scale families* follow.

While there are many approaches to learning how to play the guitar, the information contained within this book is the:

Joe Pass Approach.

Definitions:

• **Chords**...two or more notes played together at the same time.
• **Chord Inversions**...first, second and third inversions are determined by the location of the Root within a chord.
• **Chord Substitutes**...alternative chords to play that *sound* good, creating flavor and texture to songs.
• **Scale Families**...arrangement of chromatic notes (one note following the next note in a series of whole and half steps) as governed by the key signature (how many flats or sharps at the beginning of the exercise or song). These families include:

> **Major**
> **Minor**
> **Dominant**
> **Diminished**
> **Whole-tone (augmented)**
> **Half-diminished**
> **Blues**

HOW TO PLAY AND MOVE BARRE CHORD FORMS

You will be learning how to play and move chords that flow and make harmonic sense. Joe Pass uses the ***Barre Chord Forms***.

These are referred to as the ***C-A-G-E-D Forms***. All of these forms are moveable. As you move up the neck, barre the fret as illustrated on the **Chord Form** page.

All references to chords and scales in this book are in the key of "C."

CHORD FORMS

The five **Barre Chord Forms** illustrated below allow the player to move up and down the fingerboard smoothly and at the same time, be able to play vertical scales within each Form. Once notes have been played often enough and harmonic patterns, melodic lines, and scale forms have been well learned, the student will be able to interpret and improvise at will.

By barring the fret indicated and placing your appropriate fingers on the frets indicated, you can move each configuration up or down the fretboard resulting in different chords.

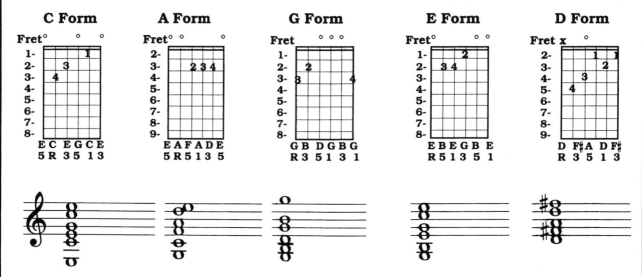

When a chord is referred to as a *triad*, the *tri* part of the word refers to **three different notes** in that chord. However, the same chord can have duplicate notes of the same tone, making one chord have four or more notes in it.

In the **C Form**, for example, six notes are being played. However, the G tone is repeated three times, The E tone is repeated twice and the C tone, twice. But there are only three different tones in the chord: C - E - G which, therefore give it the *triad* dimension.

To give the student a visual concept of how a chord looks on the guitar, we have a few chords drawn out for you. However, we must stress that it is not our intention to have the student learn the chord from the diagram only. As has been pointed out by several professional guitarists, when you enter a studio or a recording session and you have to read a chart, there will not be diagrams for you. You must know the notes, the names of chords and what notes are in them, the scales and their modifications, and, of course, the melody lines.

The diagrams listed here are merely a means to double-check yourself when you are first learning. There are literally thousands of guitar chords, most of which you will never use. Learn the essential chord families: *the Majors, minors and dominants,* and extensions and alterations will be added as you become better equipped in mastering the fundamentals.

The following three pages spell out examples of Majors, minors and dominants in the Root position: the bass note giving the identification of the chord. These are here to be used as points of reference for you. Take time to become familiar with them.

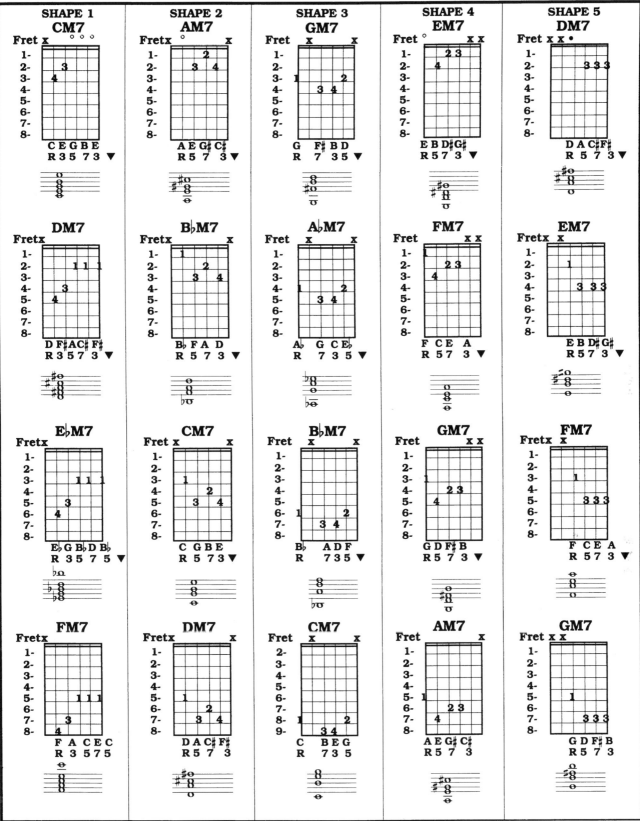

HOW TO USE THE MOVEABLE CHORD FORMS:

• 1. Select any group of four vertical chords under one column headed "**SHAPE.**" Play the first chord in that column for four beats. Change to the second chord directly under the first chord and play it for four beats. Change to the third chord directly under the second chord and play it for four beats. Finally, change to the fourth chord directly under the third chord and play it for four beats. **EXAMPLE:** Under Shape 1, play the CM7 chord, then the DM7 chord, then EbM7 and finally FM7.

• 2. Move to the second column under Shape 2 and repeat the steps above. Same for Shapes 3, 4 and 5.

MAJOR 7THS: OPEN POSITION

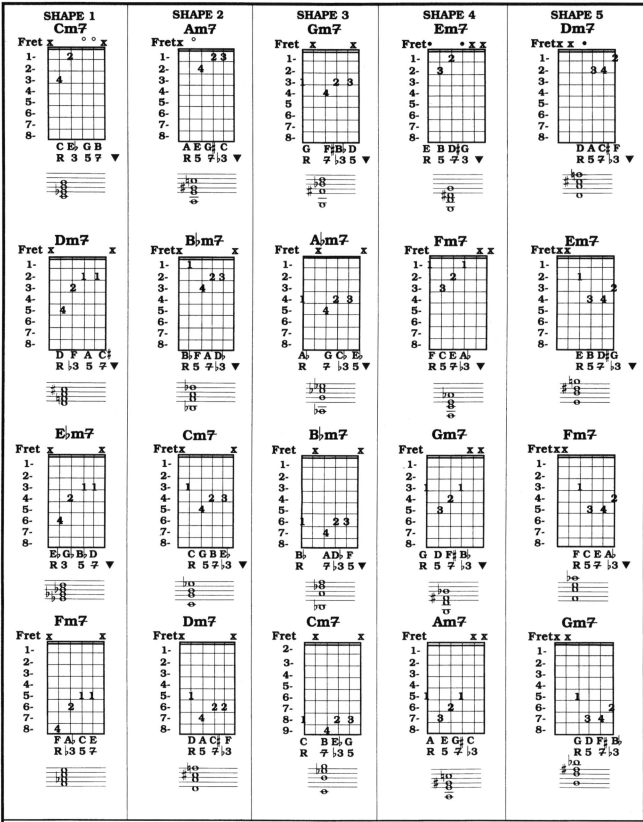

HOW TO USE THE MOVEABLE CHORD FORMS:

- 1. Select any group of four vertical chords under one column headed "SHAPE." Play the first chord in that column for four beats. Change to the second chord directly under the first chord and play it for four beats. Change to the third chord directly under the second chord and play it for four beats. Finally, change to the fourth chord directly under the third chord and play it for four beats. **EXAMPLE:** Under Shape 1, play the Cm7 chord, then the Dm7 chord, then Ebm7 and finally Fm7.
- 2. Move to the second column under Shape 2 and repeat the steps above. Same for Shapes 3, 4 and 5.

MAJOR 7TH/MINOR 3RD: OPEN POSITION

12

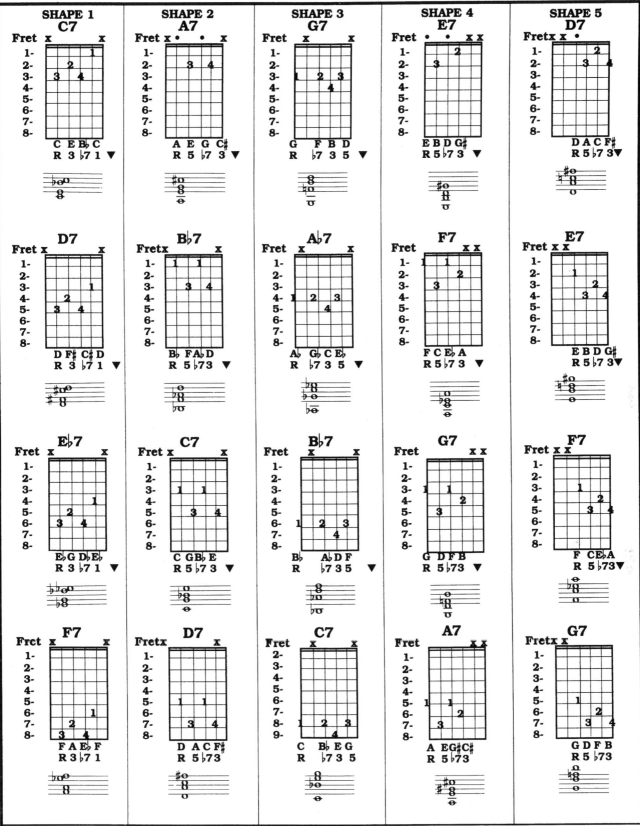

DOMINANT 7THS: OPEN POSITION

13

CHORD SUBSTITUTIONS

Chord pattern substitutions for the I-VI-II-V progression are as follows:

I = C Major 7	**VI** = Am 7	**II** = Dm 7	**V** = G 7
or C Major 9	or Am 6	or Dm 6	
or C Major 11	or Am 9	or Dm 9	

- The chords have to have common tones (most often the Root).

- For any minor chord, you can substitute a dominant chord if you're not in a minor key.

Chord substitution patterns for the chord progression (I-VI-II-V) as demonstrated above in the key of C are:

I	VI	II	V
C Major 7	A m 7	D m 7	G 7
or E 7	A +	D m 7	G 7
or E 7	E♭ 7	D m 9	G 7
or B♭7	A 7	A♭ 7	G 7
or E m	A 7	D m	G 7
or E 7+ 9	A 13	D 7+ 9	G13
or B♭ 13	A 13	A♭ 13	G 13
or E 7+ 9	E♭ 7+ 9	D 7+ 9	G 7+ 9

- Or you can use any combination of these chords to form chord pattern
  = **Chord Pattern Substitutions**
- Voice your chords with common tones in them; especially on the top strings… this makes a moving line.

JOE PASS TIPS ON VOICE LEADING IN CHORDS:

1. Chord moves with a common tone on the top string.
2. Keep chords or notes in motion, connected with voice movement or musical line.
3. Put altered notes on the top strings (G, B, E).
4. Leave the Root in the bass or omit it altogether.
5. Joe often leaves out the 5th tone note.
6. Play a ♭9 chord with the Root on the bottom. That is, put the ♭9 note somewhere *inside* the chord.

HOW TO PLAY A MOVING BASS LINE

Perhaps the signature of **Joe Pass** is his unequaled skill in playing a moving bass line. He began developing this technique as a teenager when he played in a dance band in Pennsylvania. The band leader was often without a bass player, and Joe would play bass lines on his guitar.

Fortunately for Joe, this demand from his band leader turned out to be one of his most sought after and admired techniques from aspiring guitarists, as well as his audiences in general.

While Joe tells us this is an easy technique, it only becomes "easy" after you work diligently and pay close attention to his suggestions.

JOE PASS QUOTE:

"If you can't play a bass line that's musical, you're not allowed to play that way."

To become a player who *can* play a musical bass line, do the following:

1. Play one bar of G7 (the V chord in the key of C), then one of C 7.

2. Now play a bass line, starting on a note that is in the chord you are playing.

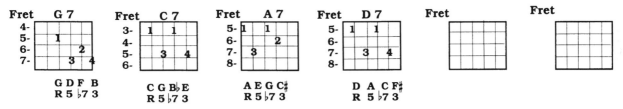

3. Play four beats (4/4 time) per measure using the notes of the G7 chord. But remember:

4. That the 5th note you play, or the **1st** note of the next measure, is to **begin** with the **Root** of the next chord named.
   ie: Under Step 2., G7, you play the notes G - D - F - **B** (which is a half-step from the Root of the next measure and chord, **C**;) C7, you play **C** - G - E - **B♭** (which is a half-step from the Root of the next measure and chord, **A**;) A7 and so on.

5. Then go back to the G7 chord and play notes in a different pattern, except that the 4th note of the measure is to be a half-step away from the first note of the next measure.

6. **It is important to remember that bass lines are linear.**

7. **It is also important to note that the notes that define a line as a linear bass line must always be a half-step above or below the note of the next measure that has a new chord.**

8. Comping on a bass line is done by playing a shuffle rhythm on every other beat (1 and 3) followed by plucking the bass line on the 2nd and 4th beats.

9. A Blues Pattern you can use to practice the Moving Bass Line may look like this:
   (Measure numbers above the chord names.)

```
1      2      3      4        5     6      7      8    9     10      11
G 7 /  C 7 /  G 7 /  D m 7  G 7 /  C 9 /  G 7 /  C 7 / F 7/ E 7 /  A m 7 / E♭9 /
12  (Turnaround) D 7 /  [G 7 - E 7 - A 7- D 7]
Repeat from G 7.
```

Photo by Jude Hibler

16

SCALES

JOE PASS QUOTE

The purpose of learning scales and arpeggios is to coordinate the right and left hands and to know where the intervals are. To learn how to hear the sounds (intervals), play slowly. Make your notes consistent, even.

When a note is unclear, a problem area, go to it and repeat it until you clear it up. This is a good way to practice.

"Play the scale from the beginning of the chord and stop when you play the last note of the chord you are playing. Then play the chord again. Play the chord before you play the scale so that you hear how it is suppose to sound. By playing the notes that way, you will have created a *line*, rather than just having played a scale."

MAJOR SCALES

There are seven notes in the **Major Scale** before the octave note is repeated. The **C Major Scale** reads:

C	D	E	F	G	A	B	C
1	2	3	4	5	6	7	8

Write out another **Major Scale:**

Write out another **Major Scale:**

Write out another **Major Scale:**

MINOR SCALES

There are three **Minor Scale** types: 1) the **Melodic Minor Scale**; 2) the **Harmonic Minor Scale**; 3) and the **Natural Minor Scale**.

The **C Melodic Minor Scale** is:

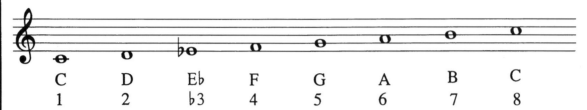

C	D	E♭	F	G	A	B	C
1	2	♭3	4	5	6	7	8

The **C Harmonic Minor Scale** is:

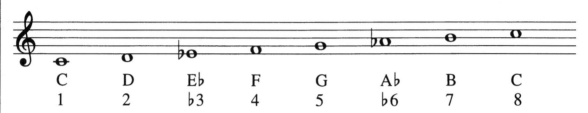

C	D	E♭	F	G	A♭	B	C
1	2	♭3	4	5	♭6	7	8

The **C Natural Minor Scale** is:

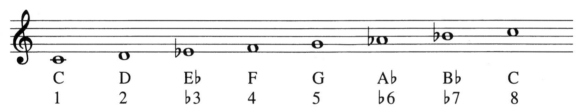

C	D	E♭	F	G	A♭	B♭	C
1	2	♭3	4	5	♭6	♭7	8

Write out another **Melodic Minor Scale:**

Write out another **Harmonic Minor Scale:**

Write out another **Natural Minor Scale:**

DOMINANT SCALES

Three of the most frequently used **Dominant Scale** types are: 1) the **Dominant Scale**; 2) the **Lydian Dominant Scale**; 3) and the **Fifth Mode Harmonic Minor Scale**.

The **C Dominant Scale (also called the C-Mixolydian mode)** is:

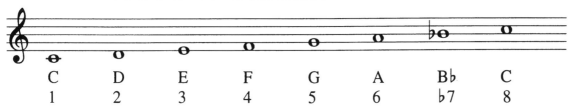

C	D	E	F	G	A	B♭	C
1	2	3	4	5	6	♭7	8

The **C Lydian Dominant Scale** is:

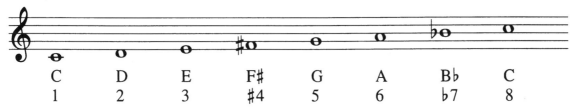

C	D	E	F#	G	A	B♭	C
1	2	3	#4	5	6	♭7	8

The **C Fifth Mode Harmonic Minor Scale** is:

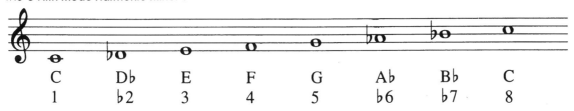

C	D♭	E	F	G	A♭	B♭	C
1	♭2	3	4	5	♭6	♭7	8

Write out another **Dominant Scale:**

_____
_____
_____
_____

Write out another **Lydian Dominant Scale:**

_____
_____
_____
_____

Write out another **Fifth Mode Harmonic Minor Scale:**

_____
_____
_____
_____

ALTERED DOMINANT 7TH SCALES
or SUPER-LOCRIAN SCALE

This scale is known by many names, but the **Altered Dominant 7th Scale** or the **Super-Locrian Scale** are most often used.

The key of C is written out for you. Following the **C Altered Dominant 7th Scale** notation, fill in the four other scales found on this page.

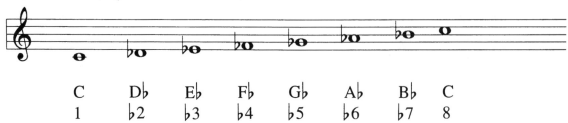

C	Db	Eb	Fb	Gb	Ab	Bb	C
1	b2	b3	b4	b5	b6	b7	8

Key of Ab

Key of Bb

Key of Eb

Key of G

WHOLE-TONE SCALES

There are only two **Whole-Tone Scales**: six notes in one set; six notes in the other.

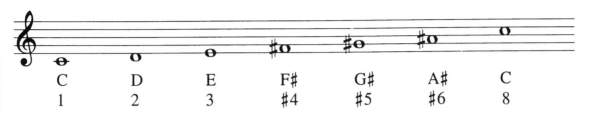

C	D	E	F#	G#	A#	C
1	2	3	#4	#5	#6	8

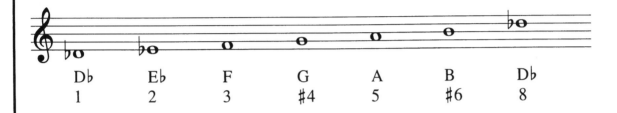

Db	Eb	F	G	A	B	Db
1	2	3	#4	5	#6	8

DIMINISHED SCALES

The **Diminished Scale** is sometimes referred to as the *Eight-Tone Scale*.
The **C Diminished Scale** reads this way:

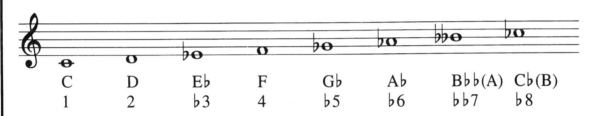

C	D	Eb	F	Gb	Ab	Bbb(A)	Cb(B)
1	2	b3	4	b5	b6	bb7	b8

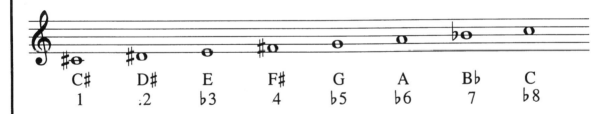

C#	D#	E	F#	G	A	Bb	C
1	2	b3	4	b5	b6	7	b8

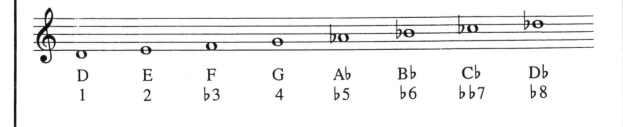

D	E	F	G	Ab	Bb	Cb	Db
1	2	b3	4	b5	b6	bb7	b8

HALF-DIMINISHED SCALES

The **Half-Diminished Scale** is also called the *Locrian Scale*.

The **C Half-Diminished Scale** is:

C	Db	Eb	F	Gb	Ab	Bb	C
1	b2	b3	4	b5	b6	b7	8

Write out another **Half-Diminished Scale:**

Write out another **Half-Diminished Scale:**

Write out another **Half-Diminished Scale:**

Write out another **Half-Diminished Scale:**

BLUES SCALES

Typically, there are six notes in the **Blues Scale** (The 1 or R of the scale, in this case C, begins and ends the scale but is only counted as one note, rather than two). It's an option to think of the ♯4 as a ♭5.

The **C Blues Scale**:

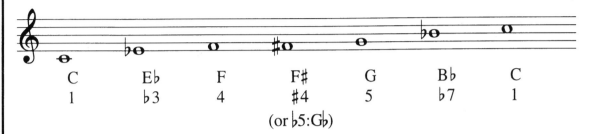

C	E♭	F	F♯	G	B♭	C
1	♭3	4	♯4	5	♭7	1
			(or ♭5:G♭)			

Write out any **Blues Scale** here:

Write out another **Blues Scale** here:

Write out another **Blues Scale** here:

Write out another **Blues Scale** here:

RHYTHM

Joe Pass on *Rhythm*: The key to accompanying singers is to *listen to them!*

"Learn and use pull-ons, hammer-ons, slurs and slides because they make your lines sound more interesting. Learn to make smooth transitions from chords and scales.

"If you are playing for a singer who does not improvise, play simply. Stay with the same voicing and movements. Good singers don't need you to play exactly the same all the time.

" The alternate picking style does not get as good a jazz sound as does the down stroke. The back picking is not as strong; it does not have the punch on the 2nd and 4th beats."

Rhythm is the principle of making musical sense through the combination of chords and scales together.

Picking techniques are as varied as there are guitarists who play. Size and shape of guitar picks vary greatly, also. Joe often breaks an already small pick in half and uses the point of that small piece. He is not as concerned with the "brand" name of a pick as he is, as with everything else involved in his music, the *sound.* Does the pick give him the *sound* he is listening for?

When he is not using the pick, he uses his fingers to play. During solos, he often uses his fingers together as a plectrum; or strums, or alternately picks strings. When he is comping (accompanying), he uses the same techniques, depending upon the style of song and the effect he wants to create.

Using the fingernails in the style of the great classical guitarists that Joe admires so much, such as André Segovia, John Williams or Julian Breem, is an art unto itself and requires special study and a lifetime of practice in order to perfect. There are many books that speak to that particular art and can be found in the *Mel Bay Music Books* catalog.

The most used guitar techniques by the fretboard hand include the:

• Hammer-ons
• Pull-offs
• Slurs
• Glissandos

JUDE'S BLUES

by Joe Pass © 1989

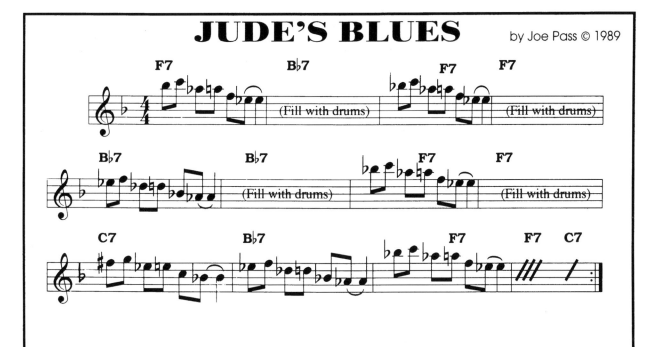

HOW TO PRACTICE THE BLUES

1. IMPROVISING ON A G 7 CHORD (The V chord in the key of C is the G 7 chord, or Dominant 7 chord, is often referred to as the "blues" chord.) You can play any of the dominant scale notes but you have to land on any strong tone of the chord at the end of a measure. The strong tones of a dominant 7th chord are the R, 5, ♭7 and 3. Write out your own Blues line in the 8 measures below:

2. PLAY EVERY CHROMATIC NOTE IN THE SCALE and then use these notes in your improvising motifs. Resolve to any of the key (strong) tones. You can play any notes of the scale.
JOE PASS: "BUT YOU HAVE TO PLAY SOMETHING MUSICAL, NOT JUST SCALES."
A motif, or musical design comes from one idea you have and then developing it; that is, repeat an idea in various places. You can use this method in any song. Write out your Blues line in the measures below:

JOE PASS "HOW TO" SUGGESTIONS

As one who has purchased many guitar books over the years looking for the one magical book which will unlock the mystery as to how to improvise, none gave me answers as much as did the few hours in the Jazz Masters Class with Joe Pass.

Trying to recreate the kind of excitement and "aha" learning experiences that my fellow colleagues and I had in that class is what is contained on the next few pages. Here is where Joe really came through in exemplary form for us students.

He came up with one idea after the other for making practice fun, improvising (almost) easy, and learning scales, an enthusiastic exercise in fruition, rather than futility. After employing these practice sessions, I hope you will agree.

We put these practice ideas toward the end of the book, as they are dependent upon your knowing something about chords and scales. Enjoy them!

HOW TO PRACTICE SCALES

FROM JOE PASS:
"If you want to play fast, you have to practice slow…slow and even. You have to think fast in order to play fast."

To get the *legato* (smooth and even) feeling, use hammer-ons, slurs and pull-offs. Practice these fretboard techniques while you are learning scales and chords.

1. **Scales teach you where the intervals are.** To learn scales:
   a. Play any chord first.
   b. Then play the scale that fits it.
   c. Play two octaves per scale.

For example: play a C Major 7th chord:

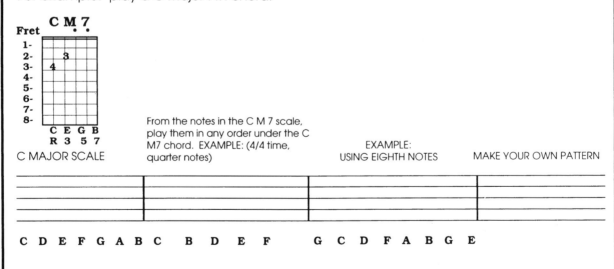

C MAJOR SCALE

From the notes in the C M 7 scale, play them in any order under the C M7 chord. EXAMPLE: (4/4 time, quarter notes)

EXAMPLE: USING EIGHTH NOTES

MAKE YOUR OWN PATTERN

C D E F G A B C   B D E F   G C D F A B G E

d. Learn intervals in the scale as a way to vary the way to practice. That is, instead of playing as the scale is spelled, C-D-E-F-G-A-B-C, play the R of the C Major 7 chord, C; then the 5th, G; next the 7th, B and finally the 3rd, E. Make up your own patterns.

REMEMBER TO PRACTICE SCALES AND CHORDS IN ALL KEYS. HEARING THE SOUNDS OF THE NOTES IN THEIR DIFFERENT SETTINGS IS KEY TO PLAYING AND IMPROVISING WELL.

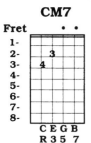

C MAJOR SCALE

From the notes in the C M7 scale, play them in any order under the C M7 chord. EXAMPLE: (4/4 time, quarter notes)

C D E F G A B C   C G B E

EXAMPLE:
USING EIGHTH NOTES

MAKE YOUR OWN PATTERN

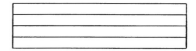

C G B E F B E C

e. Make up exercises in the scale by varying tempos; that is, the pace which the song is to be performed. Use whole notes, half notes, quarter notes, etc.

f. Practice scales at least 30 minutes per day.

2. Play one key all the way through, from C through B.
   a. Next, play the same scale chromatically.
   b. Then play five notes per string in the same scale.

3. Pick a note from the first or second strings.
   a. Then put chords to it. Play chords that have their Roots in the bass -- on the 5th or 6th strings.

b. **Make at least five different chords per note.** See the examples below. You fill in the notes.

CM7	Cm7	C•7	C7	C7+5	C13

C MAJOR SCALE

C D E F G A B C

From the notes in the C Major scale, play them in any order under the C M7 chord. EXAMPLE: (4/4 time, quarter notes)

Do the same for another chord you wrote.

Do the same for another chord you wrote.

c. Play the related scale of the chord you have chosen up to the top note that you have selected for this exercise.

d. Repeat 3 a - c with each new chord and scale you find that ends on your chosen note.

e. This exercise develops your ear to hear sounds that chords make.

_ M7

_ MAJOR SCALE

From the notes in the _ M7 scale, play them in any order under the _ M7 chord. EXAMPLE: (4/4 time, quarter notes)

EXAMPLE: USING EIGHTH NOTES

MAKE YOUR OWN PATTERN

_ M7

Fret
- 1-
- 2-
- 3-
- 4-
- 5-
- 6-
- 7-
- 8-

_ MAJOR SCALE

From the notes in the _ M7 scale, play them in any order under the _ M7 chord. EXAMPLE: (4/4 time, quarter notes)

EXAMPLE:
USING EIGHTH NOTES

MAKE YOUR OWN PATTERN

_ M7

Fret
- 1-
- 2-
- 3-
- 4-
- 5-
- 6-
- 7-
- 8-

_ MAJOR SCALE

From the notes in the _ M7 scale, play them in any order under the _ M7 chord. EXAMPLE: (4/4 time, quarter notes)

EXAMPLE:
USING EIGHTH NOTES

MAKE YOUR OWN PATTERN

HOW TO CREATE MELODIES

1. Take each Barre Chord Form, C-A-G-E-D, and play a scale under that form. By playing the C Major 7 and its comparable scales in several positions on the fretboard, you will soon be comfortable making chord and scale selections throughout the fretboard.

2. Make melodies from the forms by making phrases, rhythms with just the notes in those chord shapes. This helps visualize the chord forms.

3. Play any chord.
 a. Then start the scale from the Root of the chord and play through the scale, ending on the Root an octave away.

4. The key to playing and for getting your fingers to play the correct intervals is to:
 a. **LISTEN** to what you hear.
 b. Train your mind to get your fingers to play what you play.
 c. Get a violin or clarinet music book and learn to read the notes. Reading is a good discipline.

5. How to make smooth transitions from chords to scales:
 a. Play a chord, such as C Major 7. Then play the C Major scale and end on E, for example, on the 2nd string. This is also the top note of your C Major 7 chord. Play the chord again.
 b. Next play the D9 chord with E on top. Play the scale, starting with the Root (D) and play to E.
 c. Then play the G13 chord. Start the dominant scale on the Root (G) and play each note to E, the top note of the G13 chord.
 d. Complete this cycle by returning to the original CM7 chord.

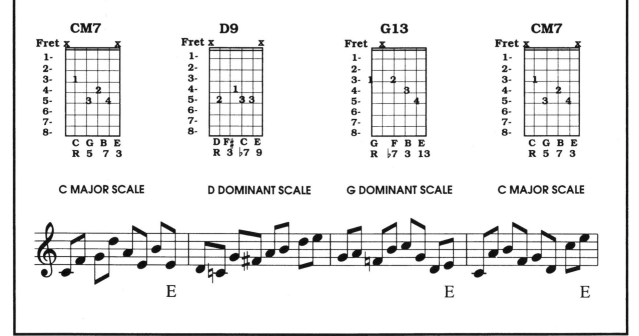

CM7 — C MAJOR SCALE
D9 — D DOMINANT SCALE
G13 — G DOMINANT SCALE
CM7 — C MAJOR SCALE

6. On the blank diagrams below, fill in your own chord patterns, followed by scale patterns as described in Step 5 a-d from the previous page.

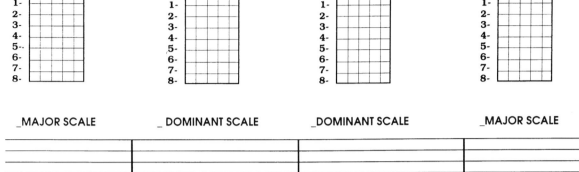

_M7   _9   _13   _M7

_MAJOR SCALE   _ DOMINANT SCALE   _DOMINANT SCALE   _MAJOR SCALE

7. JOE'S TERRIFIC IDEA...as stated by **JOE PASS** (but with a grin on his face!)

     a. To develop a practice method of becoming musical while improvising, do the following:

     b. Play a chord.

     c. Then hum a line using the sounds of that chord.

     d. Play what you have hummed. (Once your fingers have learned the scales, this will be easier as they will know where the intervals are.)

SCALE   SCALE   SCALE   SCALE

8. Tape record chords of any song. Play the chords yourself.

     a. Play only straight 8th notes continuously over the chords.

     b. Then play only 16th notes continuously over the chords, but only after you know the scales well.

     c. Hum **out loud** when playing the 8th notes. This makes your line much more musical. Test yourself as to whether or not you are actually playing what you are humming by tape recording yourself.

9. Play a song out of tempo, slowly.

     a. Put the melody on the top strings...always. (The bass player will cover the bottom notes and you want to stay out of his or her way.)

     b. Find the best chord voicings with the melody on top.

NEIGHBORING CHORDS

1. Neighboring chords is an exercise that will enhance your ability to make smooth chord changes by simply changing the position of one finger.

      a. Use three notes per chord.

      b. Work in groups of three chords using this pattern:

EXAMPLE: C7 (the V chord) to C M 7 (the I chord) to F M 7 (the IV chord).

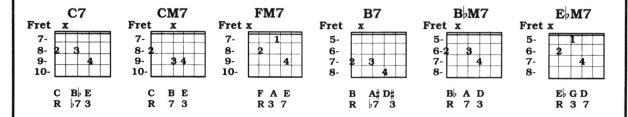

2. Play the following group of chords using the fingering patterns as shown.

      a. Then play a line over the chords.

      b. Tape record the chords you play, then vary the lines you play over the chords.

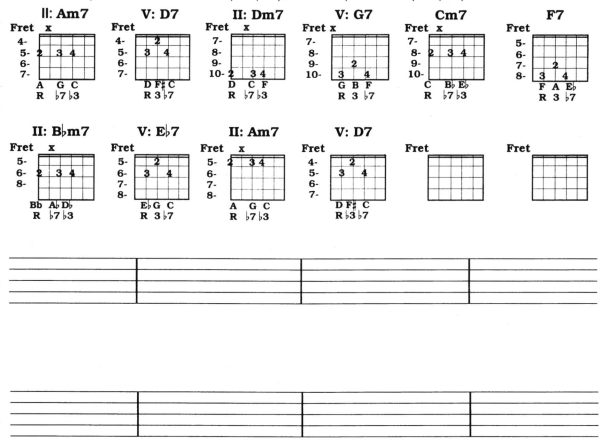

NEIGHBORING CHORDS (cont)

3. Following the pattern of Step 2. On the preceding page, use any II - V progression your own pattern, using three notes per chord.

a. On the staff lines, write out the notes that you have hummed in developing a melodic motif.

Fret II   **Fret V**   **Fret II**   **Fret V**   **Fret**   **Fret**

Fret   **Fret**   **Fret**   **Fret**   **Fret**   **Fret**

Photo by Jude Hibler

JOE PASS JAZZ PHRASES

Section One

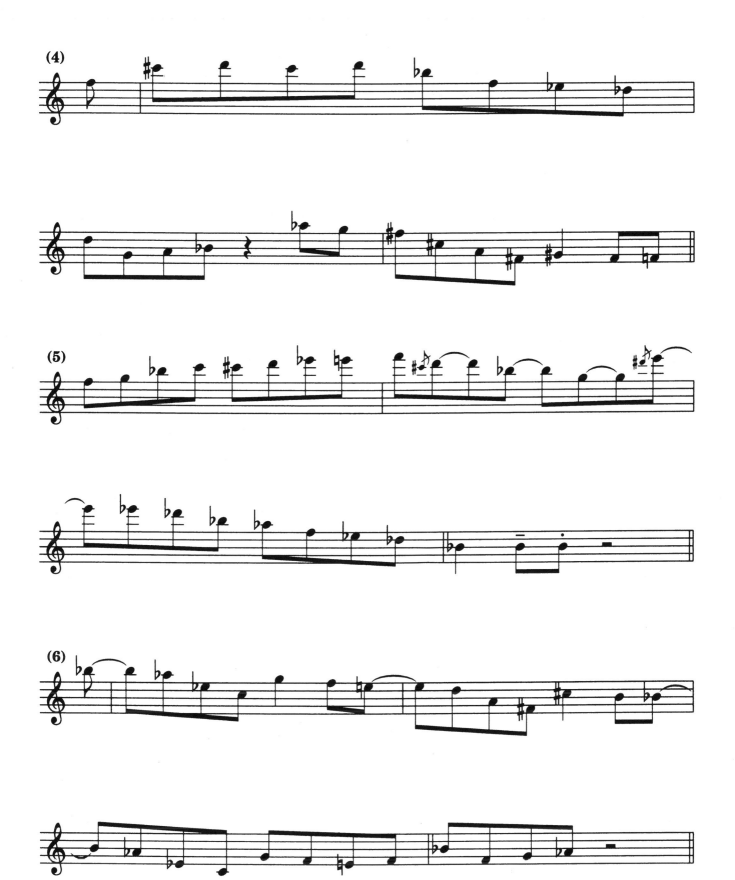

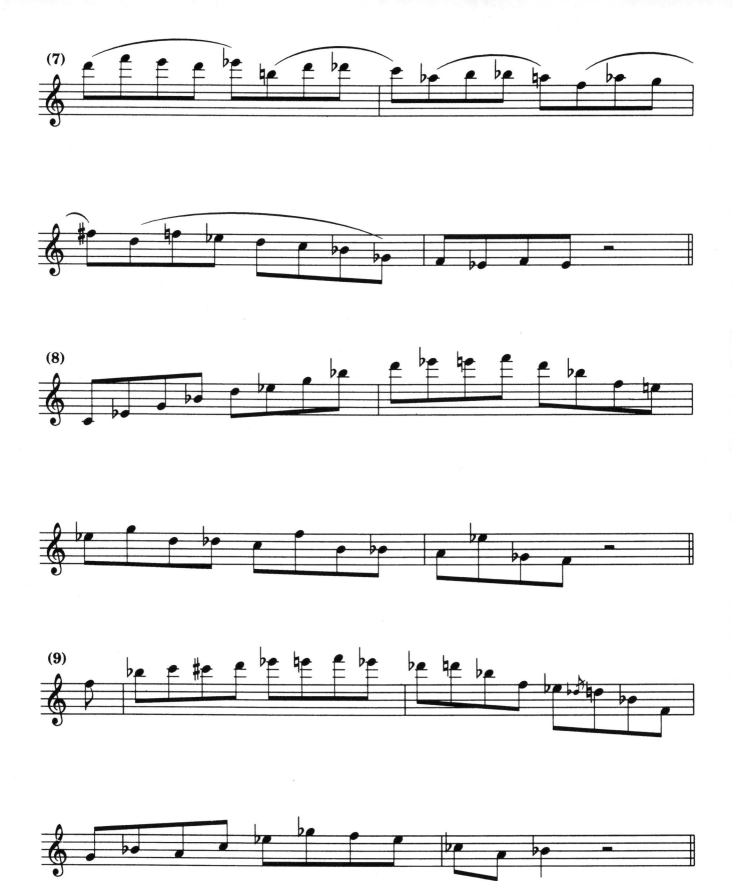

40

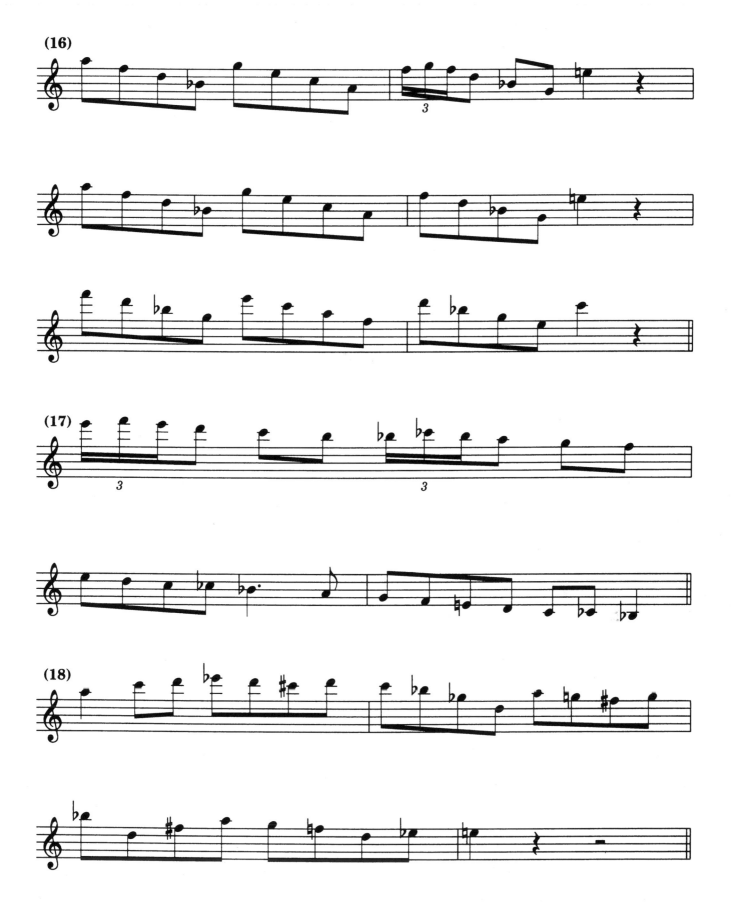

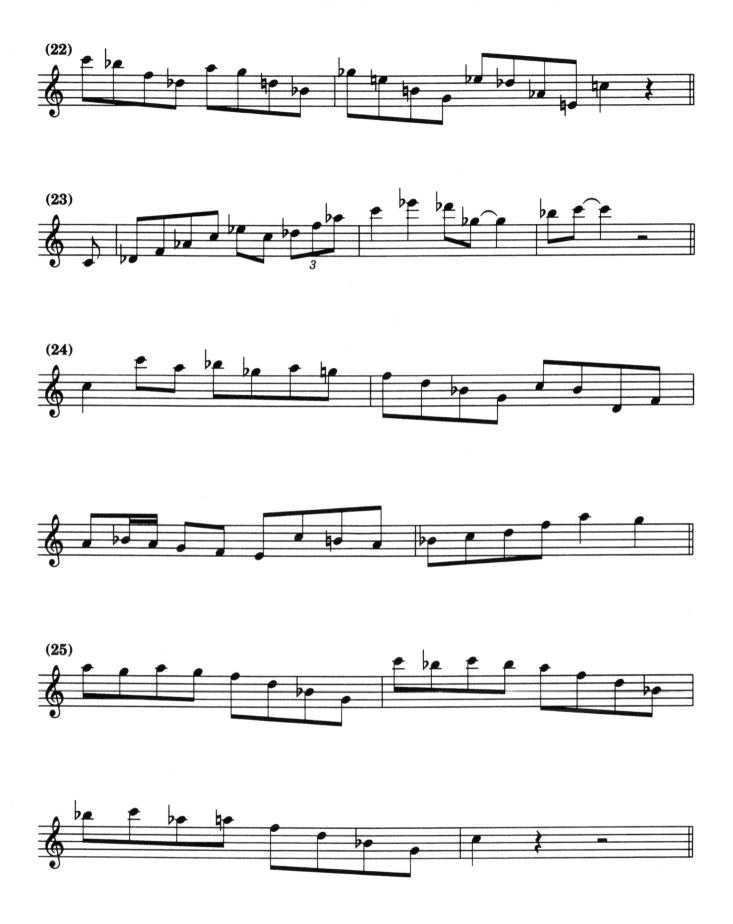

JOE PASS JAZZ PHRASES

Section Two

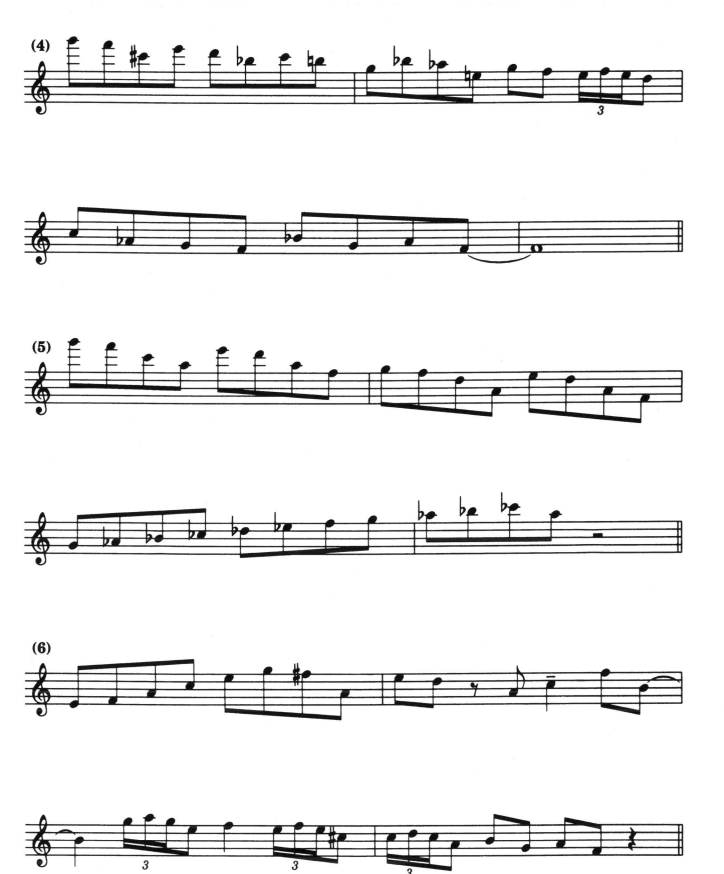

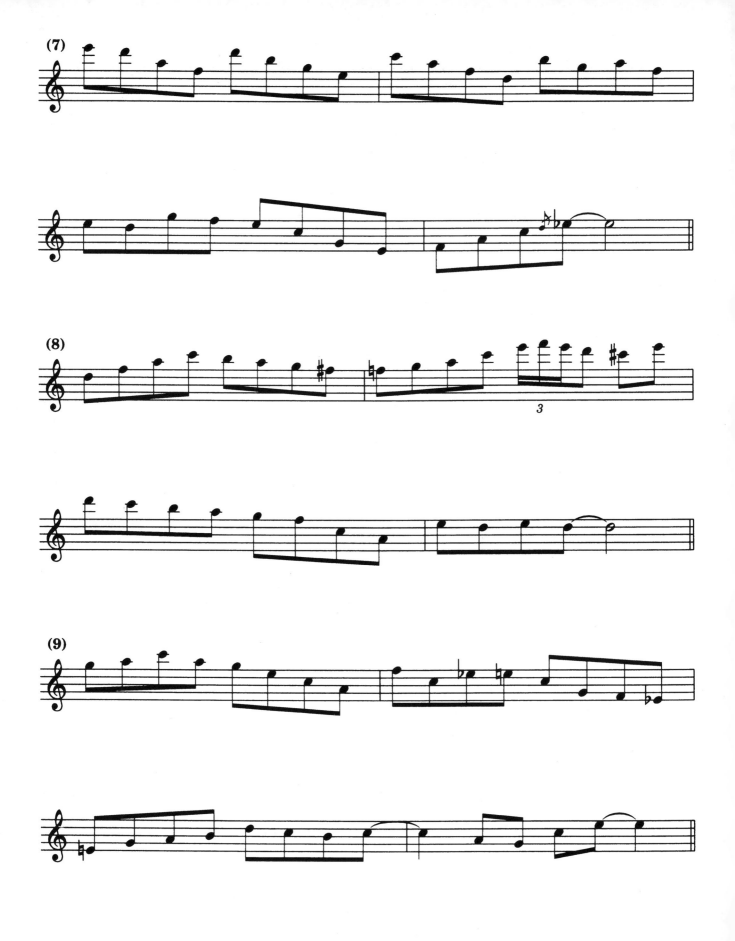

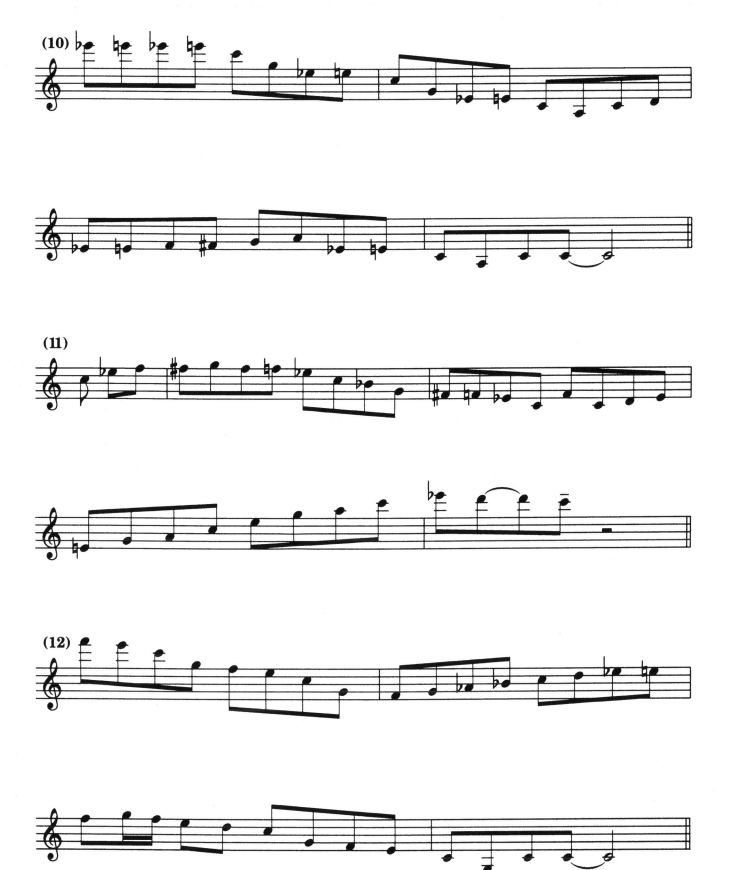

(13)

(14)

(15)

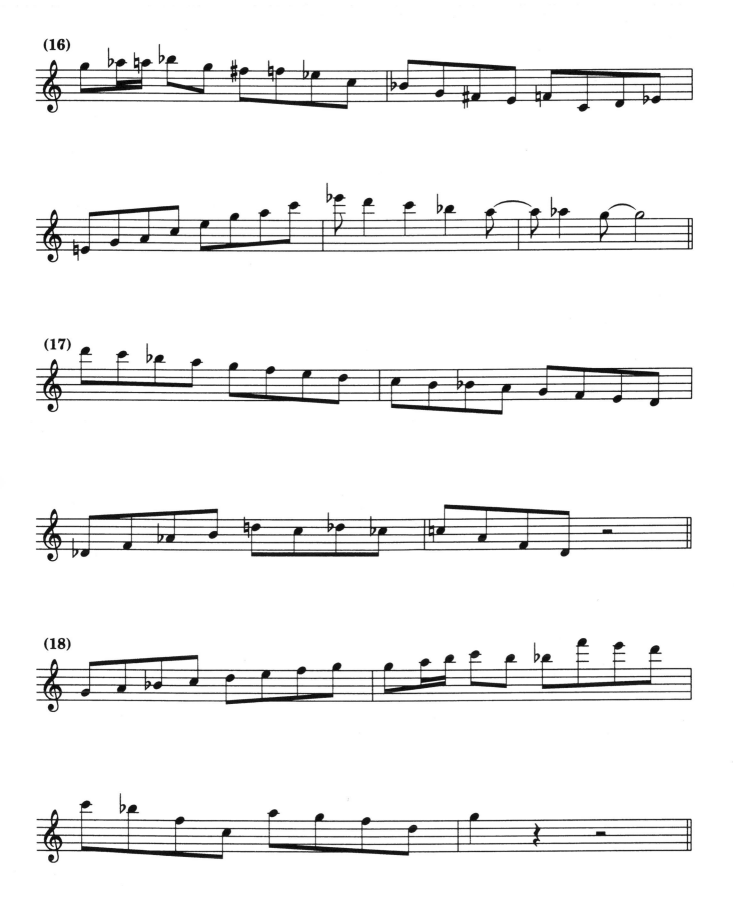

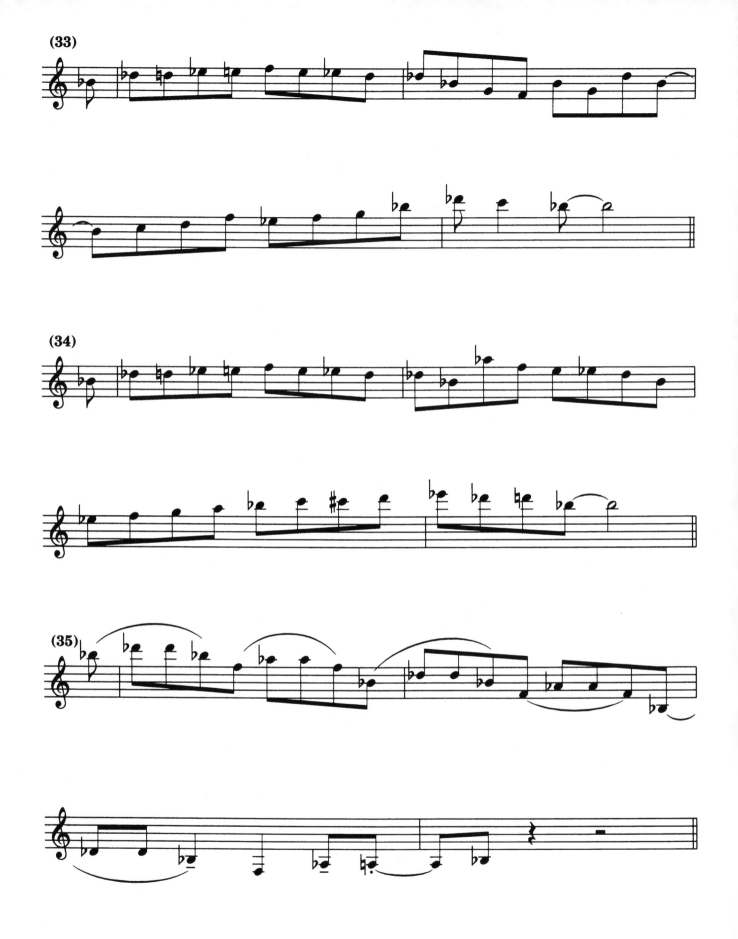

(45)

(46)

(47) May be played 8va

Photo by Jude Hibler

JOE PASS SELECTED DISCOGRAPHY

Concord Jazz: (800) 551-5299
Pablo at Fantasy: (510) 549-2500
Telarc: (800) 222-6872

Joe Pass (as leader):

Jazz (with Ray Brown, Herb Ellis, Jake Hanna)	Concord Jazz (CCD-6001)
Seven Come Eleven (with Ray Brown, Herb Ellis, Jake Hanna)	Concord Jazz (CCD-6002)
Montreux '77	Pablo (OJCCD-382-2)
Quadrant (with Milt Jackson, Ray Brown, Mickey Roker)	Pablo (OJCCD-498-2)
I Remember Charlie Parker	Pablo (OJCCD-602-2)
Virtuoso, Volumes I-III	Pablo (I: PACD-2310-708-2; II:
and Paulinho da Costa: Tudo Bem!	PACD- 2310-788-2; OCJCCD-
at University of Akron Concert	684-2)
	Pablo (OJCCD-685-2)
	Pablo (PACD-2308-249-2)
Portraits of Duke Ellington (with Ray Brown, Bobby Durham)	Pablo (PACD-2310-716-2)
Whitestone (with John Pisano, Don Grusin, Harvey Mason,	
Abraham Laboriel, Nathan East, Paulinho da Costa, Armando Compean)	Pablo (PACD-2310-912-2)
Blues for Fred	Pablo (PACD-2310-946-2)
One for My Baby (with Plas Johnson, Gerald Wiggins, Andy Simpkins, Tootie Heath)	Pablo (PACD-2310-936-2)
Summer Nights (with John Pisano, Jim Hughart, Colin Bailey)	Pablo (PACD-2310-939-2)
Appassionato (with John Pisano, Jim Hughart, Colin Bailey)	Pablo (PACD-2310-946-2)
The Best of Joe Pass (with Oscar Castro-Neves, Don Grusin, Octavio Bailly,	
Niels-Henning Ørsted Pedersen, Ray Brown, Claudio Sion, Bobby Durham,	
Martin Drew, Paulinho da Costa)	Pablo (PACD-2405-419-2)
Live at Yoshi's (with John Pisano, Monty Budwig, Colin Bailey)	Pablo (PACD-)
My Song (w John Pisano, Tom Ranier, Jim Hughart, Colin Bailey)	Telarc (CD-83326)

Joe Pass with others:

Benny Carter/Dizzy Gillespie: *Carter, Gillespie, Inc.*	Pablo (OJCCD-682-2)
Benny Carter: *The King*	Pablo (PACD-2310-768-2)
Benny Carter Meets Oscar Peterson	Pablo (PACD-2310-926-2)
Benny Carter: *My Kind of Trouble*	Pablo (PACD-2310-935-2)
Ella Fitzgerald/Count Basie/Joe Pass: *Digital III at Montreux*	Pablo (PACD-2308-223-2)
Ella Fitzgerald/Joe Pass: *Take Love Easy*	Pablo (PACD-2310-702-2)
Ella Fitzgerald/Joe Pass: *Fitzgerald & Pass...Again*	Pablo (PACD-2310-772-2)
Ella Fitzgerald/Joe Pass: *Speak Love*	Pablo (PACD-2310-888-2)
Ella Fitzgerald/Joe Pass: *Easy Living* (1986 Grammy nominee)	Pablo (PACD-2310-921-2)
Ella Fitzgerald: *The Best Is Yet to Come*	Pablo (PACD-2312-138-2)
Ella Fitzgerald: *Ella Abraca Jobim*	Pablo (PACD-2630-201-2)
Niels-Henning Ørsted Pedersen: *The Eternal Traveler*	Pablo (CASS-52310-910)
Oscar Peterson Trio w Joe Pass/Niels-Henning Ørsted Pedersen: *The Good Life*	Pablo (OJCCD-627-2)
Oscar Peterson/Niels-Henning Ørsted Pedersen/Joe Pass: *The Trio*	Pablo (PACD-2310-701-2)
Oscar Peterson Four: *If You Could See Me Now*	Pablo (PACD-2310-918-2)
Oscar Peterson/Harry "Sweets" Edison/Eddie "Cleanhead" Vinson/Joe Pass	Pablo (PACD-2310-927-2)
Oscar Peterson *Live*	Pablo (PACD-2310-940-2)
Oscar Peterson/Joe Pass: *Porgy and Bess*	Pablo (PACD-2310-779-2)
Oscar Peterson: *Time After Time*	Pablo (PACD-2310-947-2)
André Previn/Joe Pass/Ray Brown: *After Hours*	Telarc (CD83302)
Zoot Sims/Joe Pass: *Blues for Two*	Pablo (OJCCD-635-2)
Zoot Sims and the Gershwin Brothers	Pablo (OJCCD-444-2)
Sarah Vaughan: *A Celebration of Duke*	Pablo (OJCCD-605-2)
Sarah Vaughan: *How Long Has This Been Going On?*	Pablo (PACD-2310-821-2)
Sarah Vaughan: *Duke Ellington Songbook One*	Pablo (PACD-2312-111-2)
Sarah Vaughan: *Duke Ellington Songbook Two*	Pablo (PACD-2312-116-2)
Sarah Vaughan: *Crazy and Mixed Up*	Pablo (PACD-2312-137-2)

Made in the USA
Las Vegas, NV
26 November 2021

35324034R00037